# GOLFtoons

PLAINSMAN PUBLICATIONS LTD.

Published and distributed in Canada by
Plainsman Publications Ltd.
2133 Quebec Street
Vancouver, B.C. V5T 2Z9

Simultaneously published in the U.S. by
Jolex Inc., Oakland, New Jersey and
distributed by John Olson Company
294 West Oakland Avenue
Oakland, New Jersey 07436

Vertrieb für Europa:
Journal-Verlag Schwend GmbH
Schwaebisch Hall, W. Germany

First printing: 1977
Second printing: 1978
Third printing: 1980

Printed in the U.S.A.
ISBN: 0-89149-037-X

COUNTDOWN,
10-9-8-7
6-5-4-

THIS BOOK IS DEDICATED
TO INGEBORG, MY WIFE,
WHO SWINGS AND PUTTS
ALONG WITH ME,
THE SUNSHINE OF MY LIFE.

Many thanks to Betty Carter and Duke Ward
who were a great help to me.

**PLEASE DON'T TELL ME!**

I cringe when people say to me,
"You really topped that shot."
I've played golf long enough to see
How far I really got.

I manage when people say to me,
"You sliced that shot a bit."
I've played golf long enough to see
It was a lousy hit.

I dislike when people say to me,
"Your ball went in the sand."
I've played golf long enough to see
Where balls by nature land.

I hate when people say to me,
"Your chip shot was too light."
I've played golf long enough to see
The flag is not in sight.

I loathe when people say to me,
"Your putt went by the hole."
I've played golf long enough to see
I'd overlooked the roll.

I scream when people say to me,
"You had a dandy score —
A 61 and 63 ... a hundred twenty-four!"
I've played golf long enough ... Period ... (SPLASH)

*Lo Linkert*

CHICKEN!!!

GOLF AND POST OFFICES
HAVE SOMETHING IN COMMON,
IT DOESN'T MATTER HOW WELL
YOU ADDRESS A BALL OR A
PARCEL, YOU MAY NEVER
FIND IT AGAIN.

" TELL YOUR WIFE TO LEAVE THE FLOWER-
PICKING TILL LATER, OR THE BET IS OFF!"

BAN THE
DUFFERS!

" DUKE YOU'RE A LOUSY LOSER AND A
MALE CHAUVINIST PIG."

GOLF IS A GAME IN WHICH YOU HAVE TO
KEEP YOUR HEAD DOWN AND YOUR
SPIRIT UP.

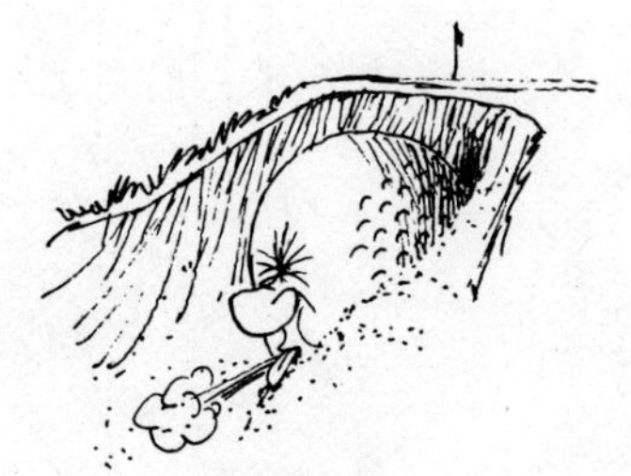

"NICE SHOT, TOO BAD IT'S THE WRONG DIRECTION."

DON'T WORRY IF YOU BLOW 18 HOLES;
THE 19th WILL MAKE UP FOR IT.

"NOW WATCH HIM COME OUT SMELLING
LIKE ROSES."

"IT'S FOR YOU FATHER."

GOLF MAY NOT BE THE GREATEST
EXERCISE, BUT IT BEATS GARDENING
BY 18 GOOD REASONS.

YOU
PROMISED
TO CUT THE
LAWN.

"I HATE TO TELL YOU, BILL, BUT YOUR STANCE IS ALL WRONG!"

GOLF AND SEX HAVE SOMETHING
IN COMMON; BEFORE YOU REALLY
MASTER IT YOU'RE TOO OLD TO BE
GOOD AT IT.

"... AND ON THE 6TH HOLE I MISSED
A SURE BIRDIE...THEN ON THE 7TH..."

I'D RATHER BE A SAD SLICER
THAN A HAPPY HOOKER.

WHAT'S IN IT FOR ME, IF I DROP FOR A BIRDIE?

WHEN A SCOTSMAN IN YOUR FOURSOME
LOSES A BALL, YOU'RE A THREESOME.

HELP!
QUICK SAND

"WHAT FLYING SAUCER?"

AN EASY WAY TO LOSE A
GOLFING FRIEND IS WHEN
YOU ASK HIM, "WHAT'S YOUR
SANDYBAG?"

STOP THAT,
IT TICKLES!

1  395 YDS PAR 4
18
19
Jo Finkett

IF YOU CAN KEEP YOUR LEFT ARM
STRAIGHT FOR 18 HOLES, YOU'RE
ENTITLED TO BEND IT AT THE 19th

1
495 YDS
PAR 5

IF I HAVE TO LOSE TO PROVE I'M
A GOOD SPORT, I'D RATHER WIN.

THE FIRST 20 YEARS IN GOLF ARE THE HARDEST. AFTER THAT IT'S ALL DOWNHILL.

1
2
3
4

" HAVE YOU GOT ANOTHER TEE, I LOST
MINE IN THE ROUGH."

HI, THERE!

1
350 YDS
PAR 3

IN LIFE NOTHING IS PERFECT,
IF YOU THINK YOU'VE GOT YOUR
GOLF GAME TOGETHER YOUR
MARRIAGE FALLS APART.

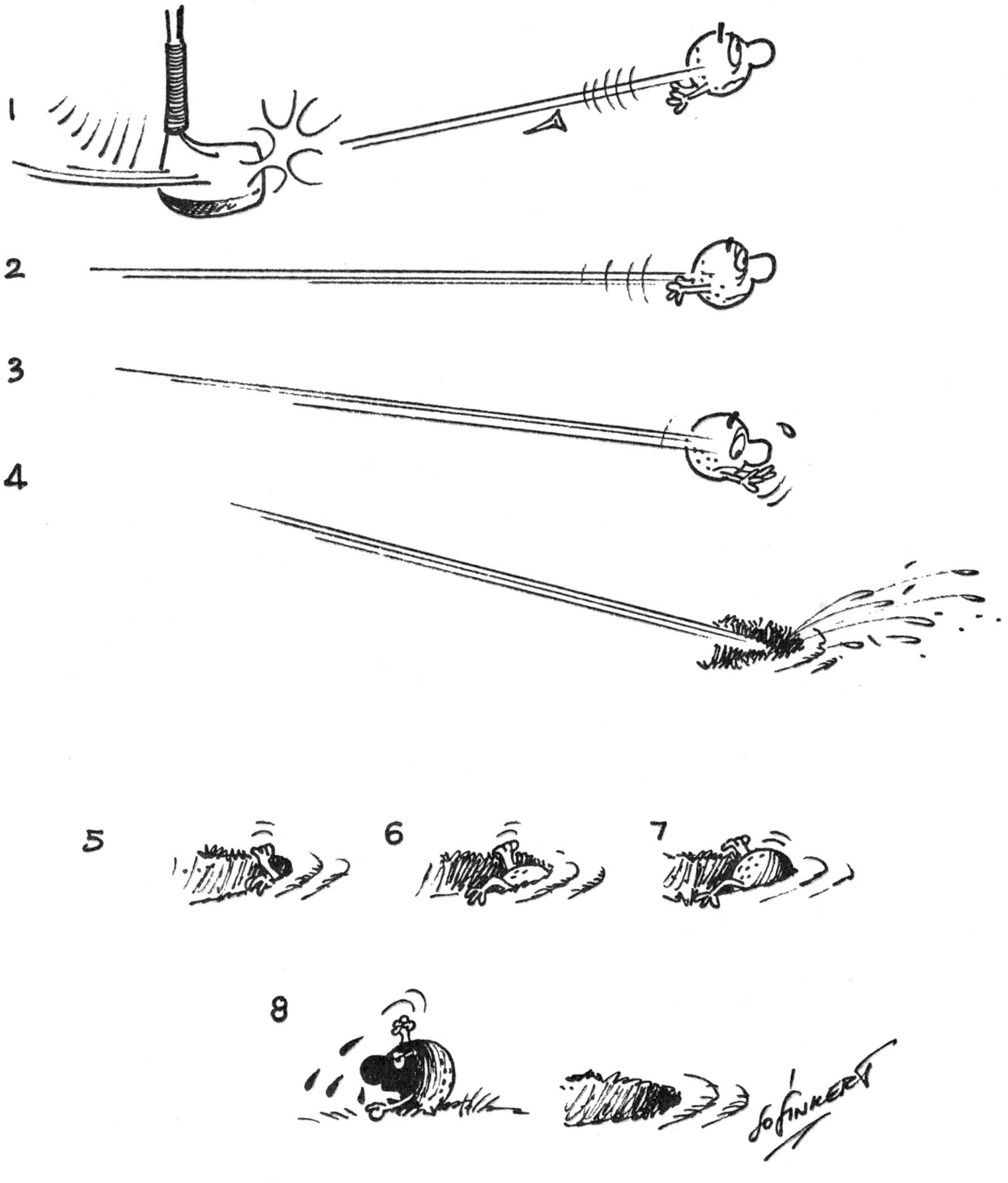

IF YOU START GOLF YOU'RE HOOKED
FOREVER. IF YOUR GAME IS LOUSY
YOU WANT TO PROVE TO THE WORLD
THAT YOU'RE NOT THAT STUPID,
AND IF YOUR GAME IS GREAT YOU
WANT TO PROVE IT WASN'T AN
ACCIDENT.

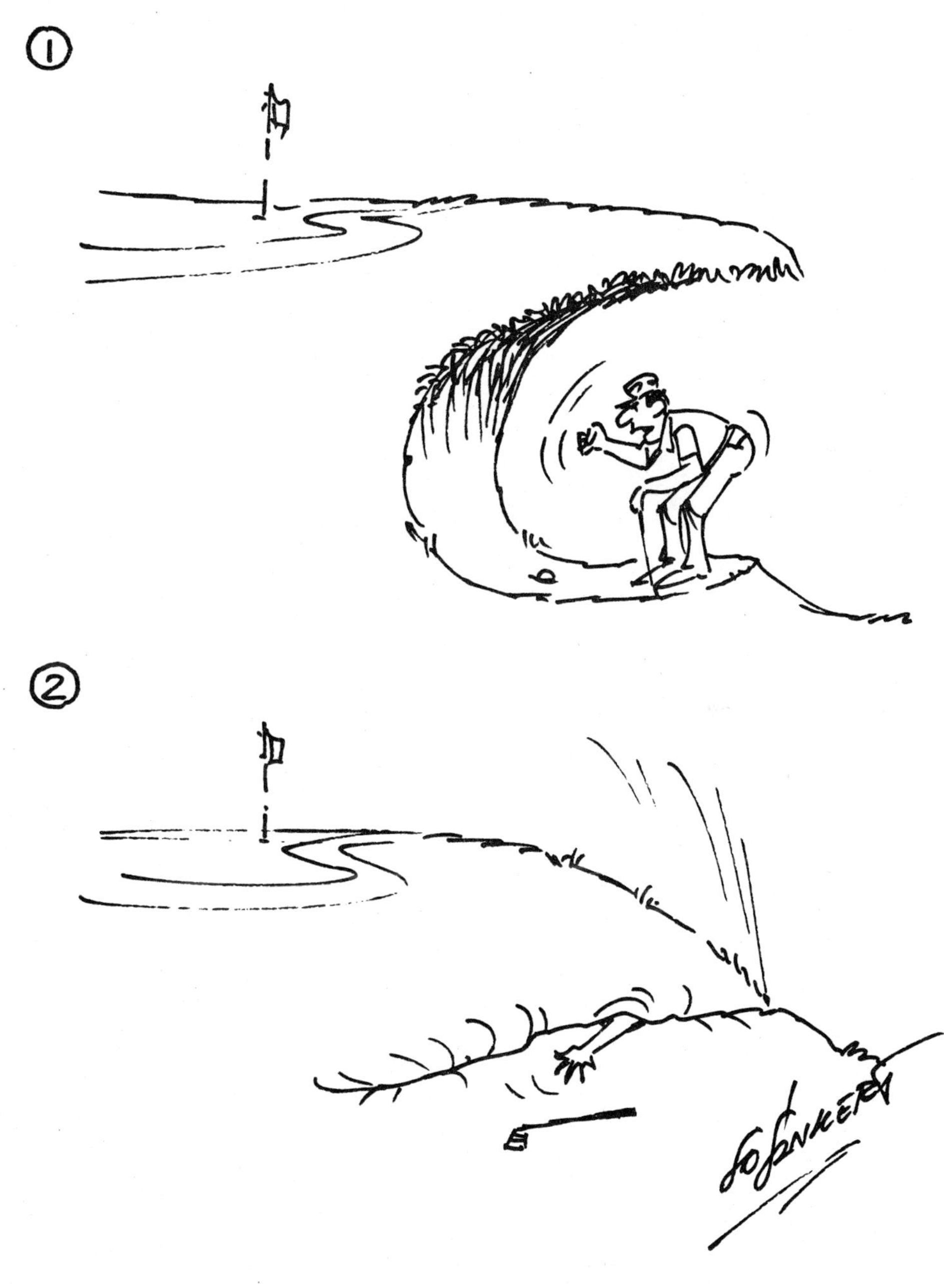

YOU CAN COME HOME NOW, JACK, MOTHER LEFT A WEEK AGO.

I ALWAYS THOUGHT I HAD THE
GREATEST ACCOUNTANT IN THE
WORLD TLL I TOOK HIM GOLFING.

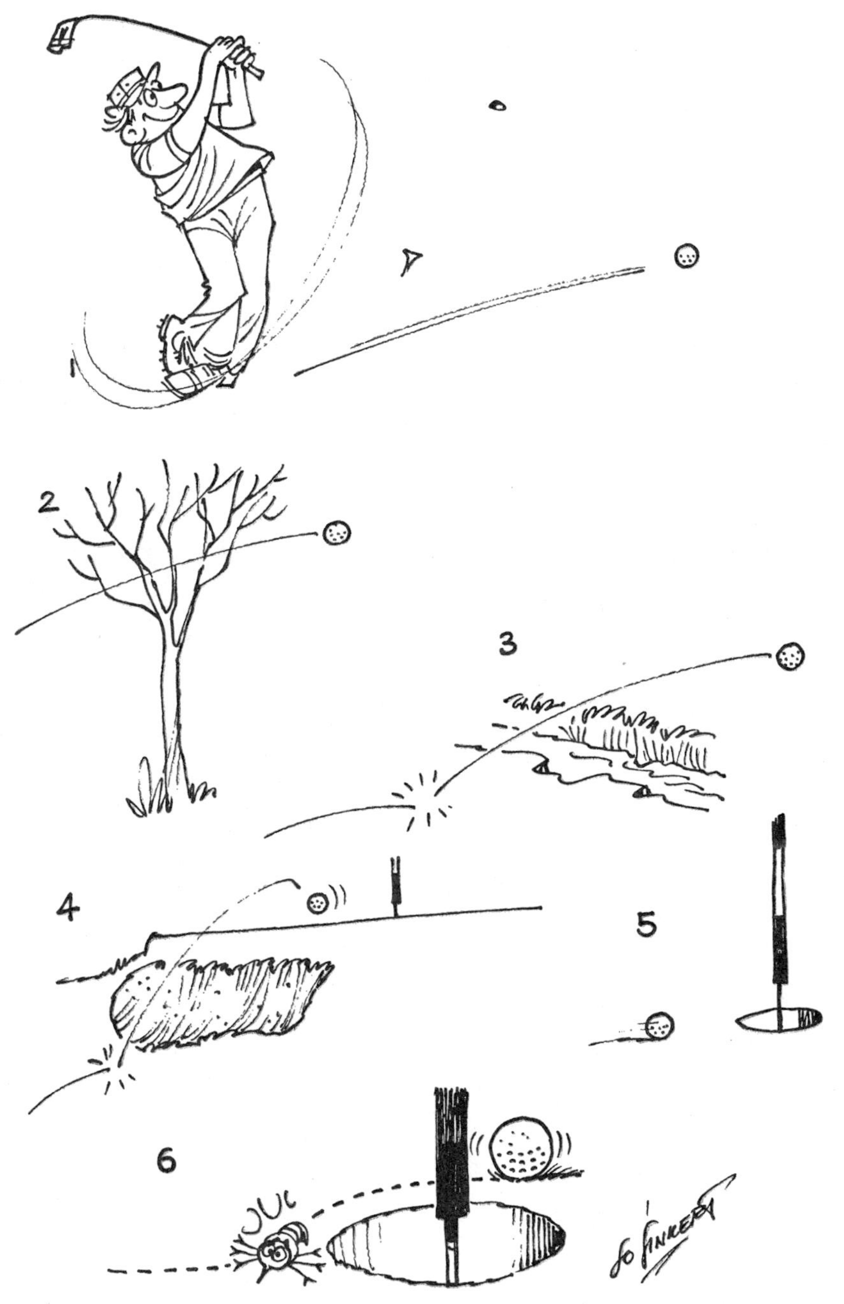

I FINALLY FOUND OUT WHY THERE
ARE 18 HOLES IN GOLF. THERE ARE
18 GREENS.

PSST, YOUNG FRIEND, IS BOBBY JONES STILL AROUND?

"BYE, BYE, JEFF, HAVE A GOOD GAME."

FIRST HE HITS
ME AS HARD AS HE
CAN AND THEN
THROWS ME IN THIS
DUNGEON.

" WE HAVE TO CUT THE DOGLEG ON THIS ONE."

GOLF IS A VERY DANGEROUS GAME,
YOU CAN EASILY GET HURT IF THE
STAKES ARE TOO HIGH.

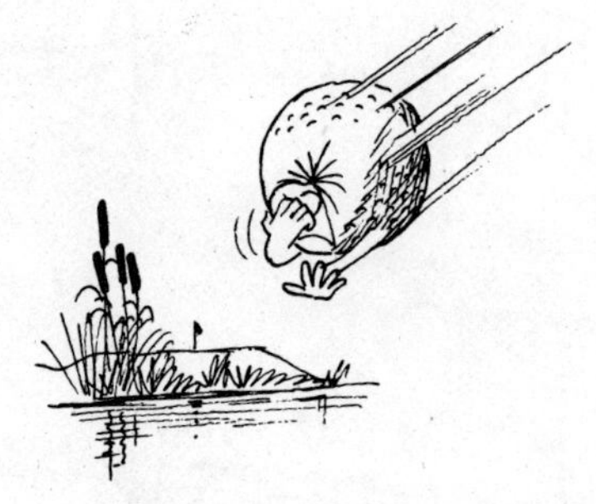

IT IS NOT POLITE WHEN YOUR FELLOW
GOLFER HAPPENS TO BE A PRIEST, TO
SAY: "GIVE IT HEAVEN, FATHER."

1
7
480 YDS
PAR 5
2
3
4
5

THANKS!
I NEEDED THAT.

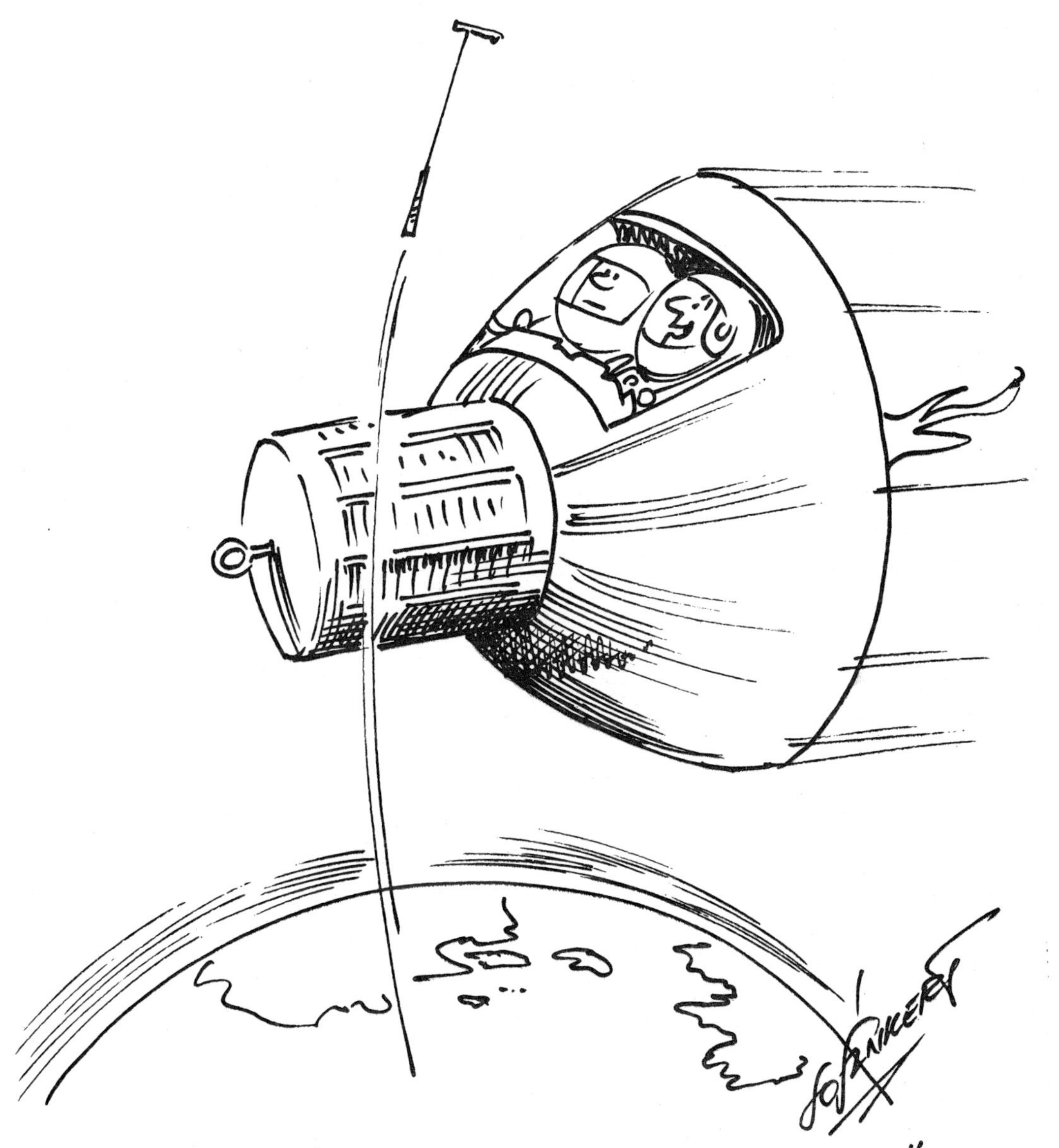

"SOMEBODY MISSED A HALF FOOTER."

SHOW ME AN ACCOUNTANT WHO KEEPS
SCORE AND LOSES AND I'LL SHOW
YOU A BUSINESS IN TROUBLE.

GOLFERS AND FISHERMEN HAVE
SOMETHING IN COMMON; THEY'RE
BOTH OUTDOORSMEN, NATURE-
LOVERS AND LIARS.

" NOW, IF YOU OVERLAP YOUR LITTLE
FINGER, WE'RE SET TO GO."

SOME GOLFERS CAN SHOOT THEIR
AGE. SO FAR I'VE MANAGED TO
SHOOT MY WEIGHT, '195'

" FRENCH OR THOUSAND ISLANDS ?"

"YOU WANT THE 'TREE' IRON, RODNEY?"

PRESIDENT NIXON MUST HAVE BEEN AN
HONEST GOLFER; IF HE WAS A SANDBAGGER
HE COULD HAVE STOPPED THE LEAK IN
WATERGATE.

WHO DO YOU THINK
YOU ARE,
HERCULES?

THE REASON THAT GOLF AND TAXES
HAVE SOMETHING IN COMMON IS: IT
DOESN'T MATTER HOW HARD YOU TRY,
YOU'LL ALWAYS END UP IN THE HOLE.

H-7017

NO, I DIDN'T KNOCK.

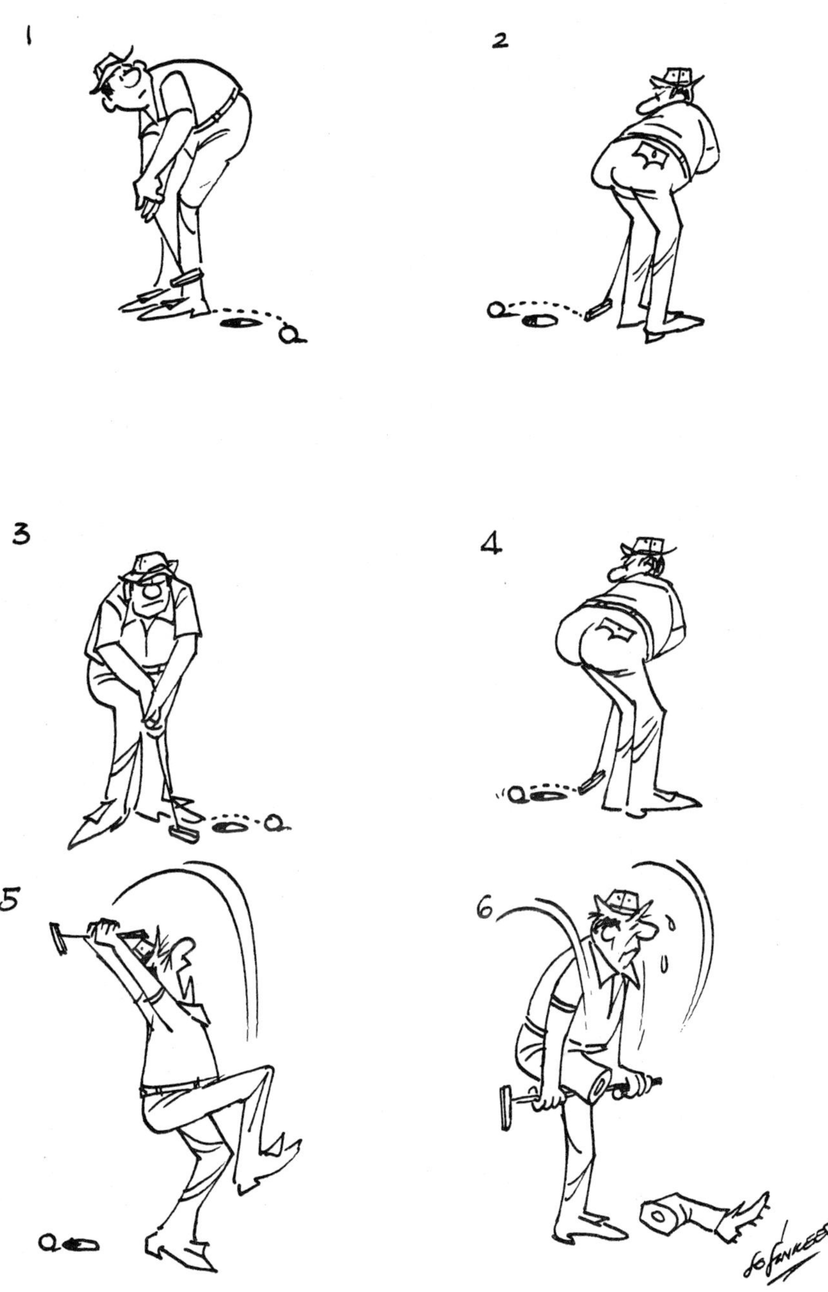
1
2
3
4
5
6

MY WIFE SAYS THERE'S MAGIC IN THE
WORD GOLF. WHENEVER ANYONE PHONES
FOR A GAME, I DISAPPEAR.

"I WAS THE ONE WHO SAID TO JACK NICKLAUS "CHANGE YOUR GRIP A LITTLE AND FOLLOW THROUGH," AND LOOK WHERE HE IS TODAY.

OUCH!!

"WATCH YOUR LITTLE FINGER ON YOUR RIGHT
HAND, GEORGE!"

I PLAY GOLF EVERY DAY OF THE WEEK,
TOO BAD THE WEEK HASN'T EIGHT DAYS.

1
2
3
4

"HE'S SO CUTE WHEN HE'S MAD."

THE EASIEST WAY TO CURE A SLICE
IS TO PUT A HOOK ON IT.

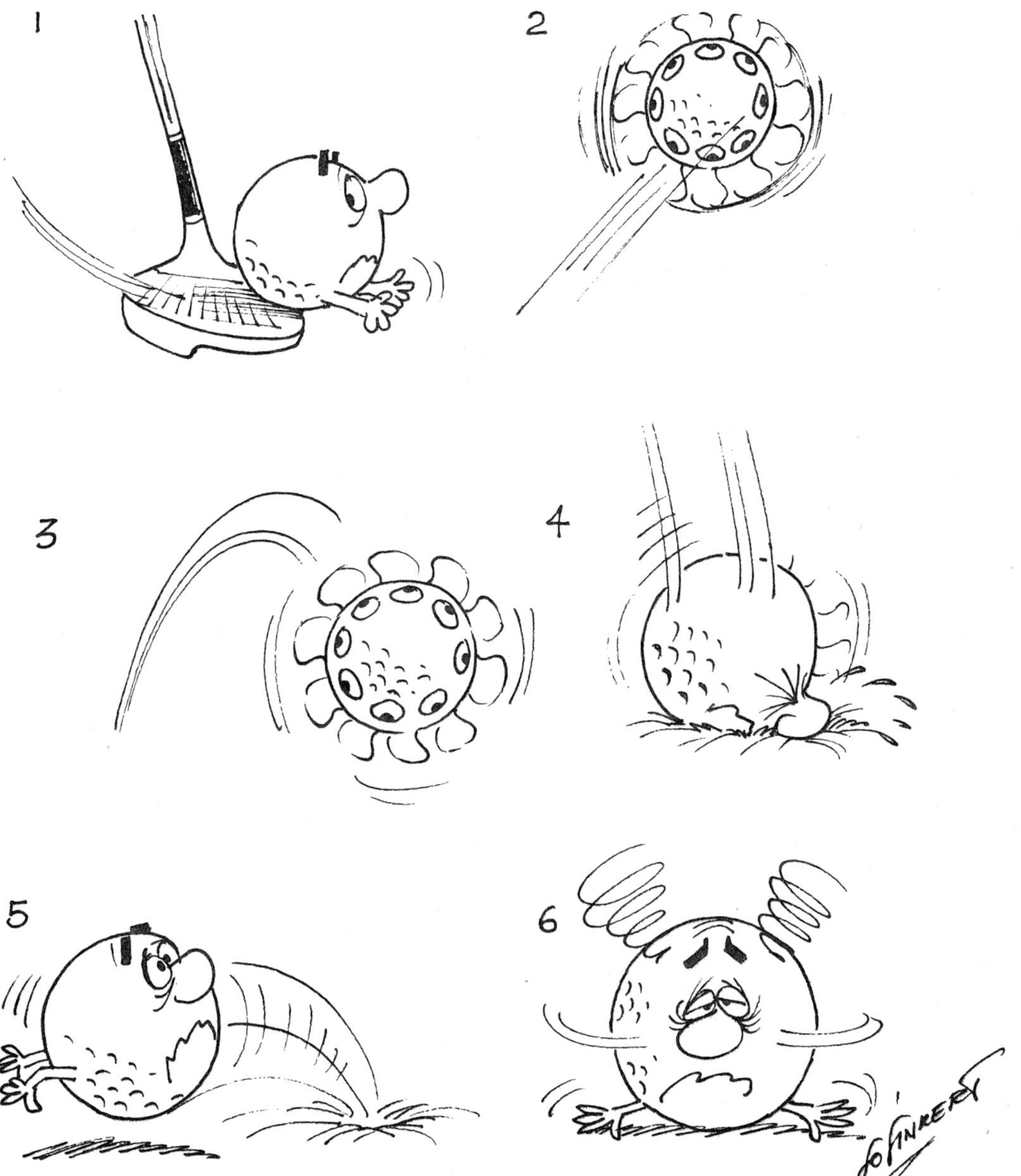

OH, ABOUT
120 MPH!

" HAVE ANY IDEA WHAT I COULD
HAVE DONE WRONG? "

BUZZ OFF STUPID, I'M NOT A FLOWER!

GIVING UP GOLF IS LIKE GIVING UP
SMOKING, YOU SAVE A LOT OF MONEY
AND GAIN A LOT OF WEIGHT.

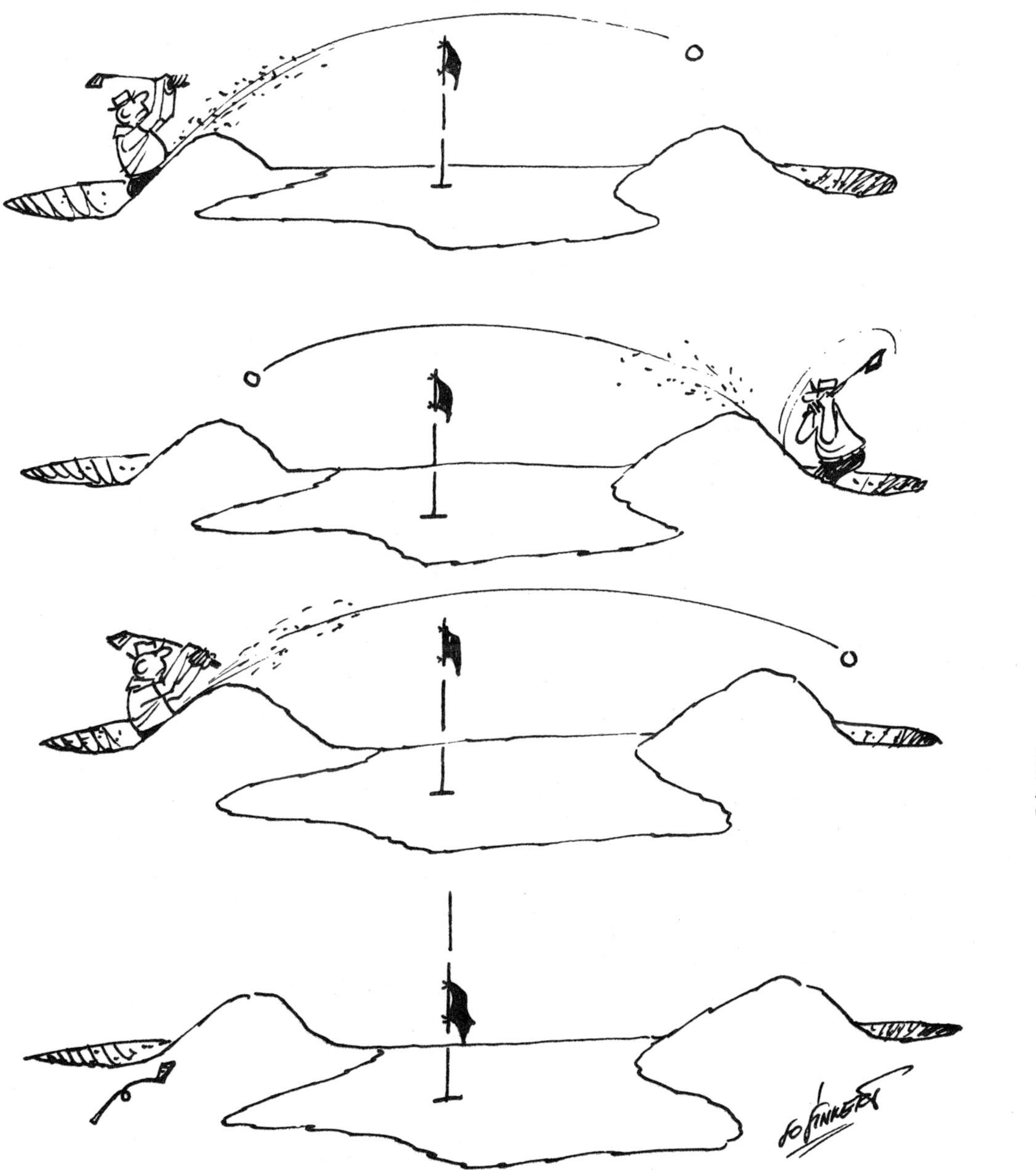

WHAT'S A NICE
GIRL LIKE YOU
DOING IN A
DIRTY PLACE
LIKE THIS?

"YOU DON'T WANT THAT ONE BACK."

GOLF IS AN ELECTRIFYING WORD, JUST
HEARING IT MAKES MY WIFE BLOW
A FUSE.

" VERY FUNNY, SHEILA !! "

THERE ARE TWO THINGS I HATE IN GOLF,
GOLFERS WHO TAKE THE GAME TOO
SERIOUSLY AND SOMEONE WHO GIGGLES
WHEN I WHIFF.

UNDER
REPAIR
STAY OFF!

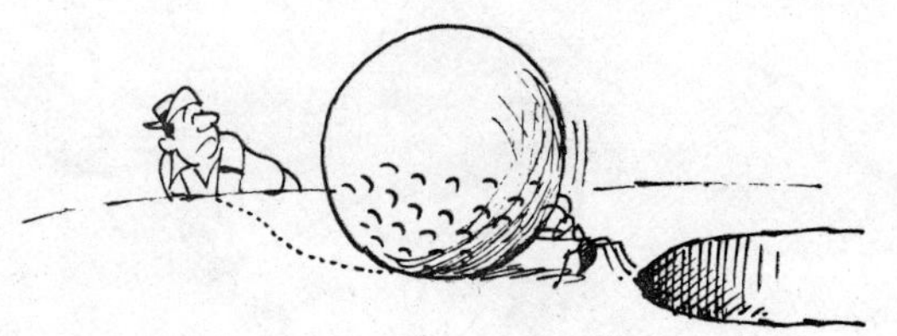

"IF THERE'S ANY WATER WE'LL KNOW
IN A SEC."

THE ART OF HITTING A GOOD GOLF SHOT IS,
SWING EASY, THEN KILL THE LITTLE RASCAL.

" SAVE THE SCORECARD FOR ME, DAVID, I WANT TO FRAME IT. "

SMILE

"FRED IS PRACTICING FOR THE GOLF SEASON."

MY PUTTING WAS SO BAD I EVEN MISSED
MY GIMMIES.

"ARNIE JUST GOT A 275-YARD HOLE-IN-ONE."

HOW CAN YOU
STILL SMILE
WITH A CUT
LIKE THIS?

HOW DARE YOU SAY I TAKE GOLF TOO SERIOUSLY. DIDN'T YOU SEE ME LAUGH WHEN I COLLECTED MY BETS?

IT'S EASY FOR ME TO KEEP MY HEAD DOWN.
I DON'T WANT TO FACE ANYONE WITH MY SCORES.

"VERY FUNNY!"

BALL
WASH